# A Helping Hand

by Judy Nayer

Modern Curriculum Press

**Credits**

**Photos:** All photos © Pearson Learning unless otherwise noted.
Front cover: Lawrence Migdale/Media Image Resource Alliance (Mira). Title page,
5: Courtesy of Guide Dogs for the Blind. 6: Courtesy of Canine Companions for
Independence. 7: Richard Sobol/Animals Animals. 8, 9, 10: Courtesy of The Seeing
Eye, Inc. 11: Courtesy of Dogs for the Deaf, Central Point, Oregon. 12: Courtesy of Lee
Youngblood/San Francisco SPCA Hearing Dog Program. 13: Courtesy of Dogs for the
Deaf. 14: Courtesy of John A. Howell/Susquehanna Service Dogs. 15: Alan
Fortune/Animals Animals. 16, 17: Courtesy of Absaroka Search Dogs of Montana. 18:
Bob Winsett/Index Stock. 19: Dennis Barna for Pearson Learning. 20: Lawrence
Migdale. 21: Courtesy of Steve Fritsche/Tender Loving Canines, Service Dogs. 22, 23:
Courtesy of Susquehanna Service Dogs. 24: Courtesy of Julie Miller for Therapet
Animal Assisted Therapy Foundation. 25: Courtesy of Susquehanna Service Dogs. 26:
Courtesy of Guide Dogs for the Blind. 27, 28: Courtesy of Randy Cohen for Therapet
Animal Assisted Therapy Foundation. 29: SuperStock, Inc. 30: BIOS (Alain
Mozay)/Peter Arnold, Inc. 31: Courtesy of Piney Hardiman.

Cover and book design by Lisa Ann Arcuri

ISBN 0-7652-1366-4

Printed in the United States of America

13 14 15    10 09

Modern
Curriculum
Press

Pearson Learning Group

**1-800-321-3106**
**www.pearsonlearning.com**

# Contents

To Matthew and Rob, with love

# Eyes

Who has helping eyes? Guide dogs do. Guide dogs help people who are blind, or can't see well.

A guide dog is a blind person's eyes. The dog helps a blind person to do things and go places.

**Guide dog with owner in restaurant**

Guide dog puppies live with families. The families take the puppies to stores, schools, and other places. They teach the puppies to do things such as sit and stay.

Then the puppies go to school. At the school, trainers teach the dogs to do more things. The dogs learn to go right and left.

A girl with guide dog puppy

Guide dogs train with a harness.

Next the dog learns to wear a harness. The harness fits over and around the dog's body. It has a stiff metal handle on the top. The blind person holds the handle. This helps the person feel which way the dog is walking.

People who want guide dogs have to go to school, too. They must learn to work with the guide dog. Trainers teach them how to tell the dog what to do.

When guide dogs finish school, they are ready to help. The dogs will help their owners get to school or work. They will help their owners get on and off the bus. They will lead their owners around things that are in the way. They will guide their owners across busy streets.

Guide dog leads a person around a stool.

**Guide dog and blind person cross the street.**

When guide dogs come to a street, they stop. The dogs' owners listen to the cars. They hear the cars stop. Then they know the light has changed. The dogs do not move yet. They wait until it is safe to cross the street.

The owner and a guide dog become a team. They go everywhere together. They do not have to ask other people to help them.

Blind people who own guide dogs are never alone. They always have their best friends with them.

A blind person with his guide dog

**Guide dogs stop working when they are about 8 years old. They might go back to the families who raised them.**

## Chapter 2

**Helping**
# Ears

Who has helping ears? Hearing dogs do. Hearing dogs help deaf people, or people who can't hear well. These dogs are trained to help deaf people know about the sounds around them.

**A deaf person gets her new hearing dog.**

**Hearing dog goes to a ringing phone.**

When the alarm clock buzzes, hearing dogs wake their owners. The dogs might do this by jumping on their owners' beds. They bring their owners to the door when the bell rings. They go to the telephone when it rings.

Hearing dogs also learn to warn their owners about dangerous sounds. The sound might be a boiling pot on the stove. The sound might be a smoke alarm buzzing.

Hearing dogs help their owners outside, too. When the dogs hear a sound, they perk up their ears. Then they turn their heads. The owners watch their dogs. They look to see what their dogs hear.

Hearing dog shopping with its owner

Deaf people use hand signals to tell their dogs what to do. The dogs learn these signals. Then dogs and their owners become a team.

Hearing dog and owner share a hug.

**People should not pet any helping dogs when they are working. They should wait for the owners to say they can.**

# Noses

Who has a helping nose? Search and rescue dogs do. Search and rescue dogs help find missing people. The dogs use their noses to look for them.

Rescue dog and owner search in snow.

Search and rescue dogs help find people who are lost. People can be lost in the woods. People can be lost in the snow. They might be hurt or cold. It is important to find them fast.

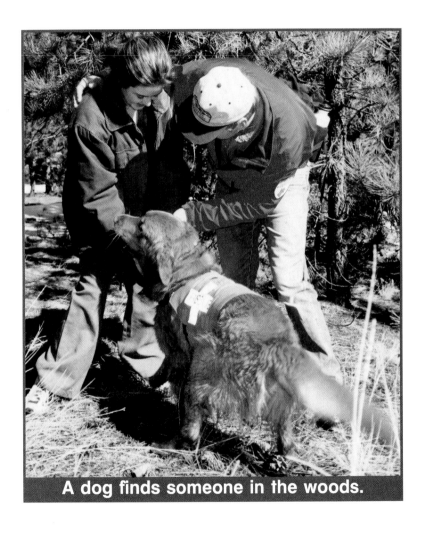

A dog finds someone in the woods.

**Some dogs rescue people in the water.**

To find someone, the dogs use smell. They sniff something the missing person had close to him or her. The odor tells the dogs what the person smells like. Then the dogs find the smell on the ground and follow it.

Search and rescue dogs have to be strong. Often they must pull people to a safe place. Some rescue dogs have to be good swimmers, too. A lot of rescue work takes place in the water.

Search and rescue dogs are trained for their job. They learn how to find people in snow. They learn to find people trapped in buildings.

Rescue work takes the dogs to many different places. Sometimes they ride in a helicopter. Other times they ride up a ski lift.

Rescue dogs sometimes ride ski lifts.

Search and rescue dogs like their work. They love to find people. They have saved many lives, too.

A girl says thank you to a rescue dog with a hug.

**More Help**

**Though many search and rescue dogs are big, they are gentle. When they find someone, they lick the person's face.**

# Paws

Who has helping hands? Service dogs do. These dogs help people who cannot walk well or are in wheelchairs. They become the hands, arms, and legs of people they help.

A service dog helps his owner.

**Service dog greets children.**

Good service dogs are smart and ready to do things for people. In a training school, service dogs learn to do lots of things. They practice helping people in crowded spots. They go to stores and places to eat.

Service dogs are trained to do lots of things some people can't do. The dogs can pull a person in a wheelchair up hills and over curbs. They turn on lights. They pick up things. They can bring things to a person. The dogs open doors. They can even push elevator buttons.

A service dog opens a door.

**A service dog helps a person shop.**

Service dogs can help people shop, too. The dogs pick up things people want to buy. They can also give the money to the store owner.

People with service dogs can live on their own. The dogs help them do a lot of things.

**More Help** Some service dogs have also saved their owners' lives. They got help when their owners were sick.

## Chapter 5

**Helping**
# Hearts

Who has a helping heart? Visiting dogs do. Many dogs are fun, loving pets. Visiting dogs are more than that. They have a special job to do. Their job is to cheer up people who are sick or lonely.

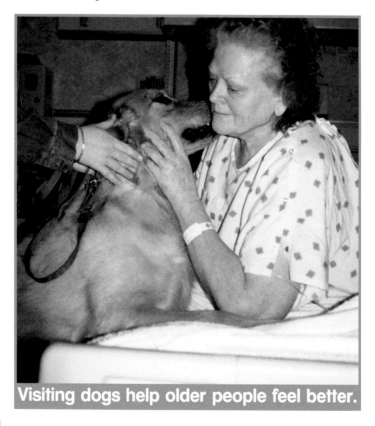

**Visiting dogs help older people feel better.**

Visiting dogs on their way for training

Many kinds of dogs can learn to be visiting dogs. All visiting dogs must be happy and gentle. They must like making friends.

Like the other dogs in this book, visiting dogs have to be trained to do their job. Many visiting dogs start their training when they are about two years old. Then they go to school.

A helping dog waits before greeting someone.

Dogs in training learn not to say hello to a person until they are told to. They learn to wait for the words, "Go say hello." The dogs meet all kinds of people. They get used to being handled and touched.

Visiting dogs visit people in many different places. They may go to a hospital for children. A visiting dog might play with a girl in a wheelchair. It might let a boy brush its fur or rub its belly. It might just lay next to someone.

**Dogs visit a sick child in the hospital.**

At a nursing home a visiting dog might cuddle in a man's lap. It might listen to a woman talk. It might play with someone.

Visiting dogs are special friends with big hearts. They help cheer up people. Sometimes a visiting dog is the best medicine!

**A dog visits a nursing home.**

**Birds, horses, cats, rabbits, and pot-bellied pigs are also trained to be visiting animals.**

# Friends

Dogs have been helping people for a long time. Many dogs help people do their work. They help people such as farmers and police officers do their jobs. Herding dogs are one kind of working dog. They make sure that sheep or cows do not wander away.

**Dog working at a sheep station in Australia**

Some dogs help pull and carry things. They might carry a backpack or pull a wagon. In places where there is a lot of snow, dogs pull sleds. These dogs can travel for many miles without getting tired.

Sled dogs run in a race.

**Dogs like to be with people.**

Most dogs seem to love helping people. The best job for any dog is being a person's good friend. A dog is happy when it can be with a person. Having a helping friend is sure to make a person very happy, too.

A sled dog named Balto led a dog team through the snow. They carried medicine to sick children in a town in Alaska.

# Glossary

**guide** [gyde] to help or lead the way

**harness** [HAHR nus] straps and metal pieces that fit around an animal's body

**owner** [OH nur] a person who has or owns something

**rescue** [RES kyoo] to save from danger

**search** [SURCH] to look for something

**service** [SUR vus] work done for others

**signals** [SIHG nulz] movements of the hands that tell someone to do something

**trainer** [TRAY nur] a person who teaches others